Up and

It is time to get up.
It is time to get dressed.

3

I put on my coat.

I put on my boots.

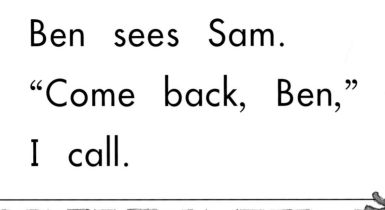

Ben sees Sam.
"Come back, Ben,"
I call.

6

Sam is up the tree.
"Sam, Sam,
come down, Sam,"
I call.

9

Dad sees Sam.

Dad goes up the ladder.

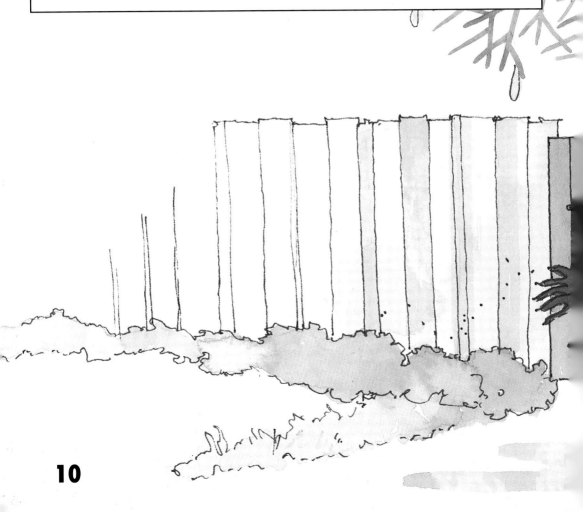

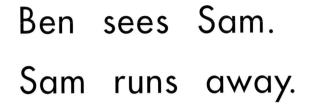

Ben sees Sam.

Sam runs away.

12

Sam is down,
but Dad is up.
"Come down, Dad,"
I call.

Sam is down.
Dad is down.
"Time for breakfast,"
I say.